SOLDIERS
OF THE REVOLUTIONARY WAR

PATRICK CATEL

Heinemann Library
Chicago, Illinois

www.heinemannraintree.com
Visit our website to find out
more information about
Heinemann-Raintree books.

To order:

☎ Phone 888-454-2279

🖥 Visit www.heinemannraintree.com
to browse our catalog and order online.

Edited by Megan Cotugno
Designed by Ryan Frieson
Picture research by Tracy Cummins
Originated by Capstone Global Library
Printed in the USA by Lake Book Manufacturing Inc.

14 13 12 11 10
10 9 8 7 6 5 4 3 2 1

Library of Congress Cataloging-in-Publication Data

Catel, Patrick.
  Soldiers of the Revolutionary War / Patrick Catel.
    p. cm. — (Why we fought, the Revolutionary War)
  Includes bibliographical references and index.
  ISBN 978-1-4329-3898-7 (hc)
  1. United States. Continental Army--Military life--Juvenile
literature. 2. Great Britain. Army—Military life—History—
18th century—Juvenile literature. 3. United States—History—
Revolution, 1775-1783—Juvenile literature. 4. Soldiers—
United States—History—18th century. 5. Soldiers—Great
Britain—History—18th century. I. Title.
  E259.C38 2011
  973.3—dc22
                    2009050075

Acknowledgments

The author and publishers are grateful to the following for
permission to reproduce copyright material:

Corbis pp. 13 (© Burstein Collection), 42 (© Bettmann);
Getty Images pp. 20, 34 (Stock Montage), 43; Library of
Congress Prints and Photographs Division pp. 4, 9, 11, 27, 30;
National Archives pp. 10, 12 (War and Conflict CD); National
Geographic Stock p. 35 (Louis S. Glanzman); National Park
Service, Colonial National Historical Park p. 24; Superstock
p. 32; The Art Archive pp. 7, 19, 37 (Chateau de Blerancourt/
Gianni Dagli Orti), 22; The Bridgeman Art Library
International pp. 8, 25, 39 (Peter Newark American Pictures),
21 (© Peabody Essex Museum, Salem, Massachusetts, USA),
26 (National Army Museum, London), 33; The Granger
Collection, New York pp. 14, 15, 16, 17, 23, 29, 31, 38, 40, 41

Cover photo of "The Nation Makers." Depicts the Battle of
Brandywine of 1777 during the Revolutionary War. Oil on
canvas by Howard Pyle, 1906, reproduced with permission
from The Granger Collection, New York.

We would like to thank Dr. Edward Cook for his invaluable
help in the preparation of this book.

Every effort has been made to contact copyright holders of
any material reproduced in this book. Any omissions will
be rectified in subsequent printings if notice is given to the
publisher.

All the Internet addresses (URLs) given in this book were valid
at the time of going to press. However, due to the dynamic
nature of the Internet, some addresses may have changed, or
sites may have changed or ceased to exist since publication.
While the author and Publishers regret any inconvenience this
may cause readers, no responsibility for any such changes can
be accepted by either the author or the Publishers.

Contents

Throughout this book, you will find green text boxes that contain facts and questions to help you interact with a primary source. Use these questions as a way to think more about where our historical information comes from.

Some words are shown in bold, **like this**. You can find out what they mean by looking in the glossary, on page 46.

Why Did We Fight the Revolutionary War?

Today, the United States of America is one of the strongest nations in the world. This makes it difficult to imagine how close the American **colonies** were to failing in their revolution. The supporters of the Declaration of Independence risked their lives in a war against the most powerful nation in the world in 1776. Why would they risk so much?

In 1760, George III became king of Great Britain. He signed the Treaty of Paris with France in 1763 to end the **French and Indian War**. The British gained control of Canada and the land east of the Mississippi River. However, Great Britain had a large debt from the war.

Fighting took place at Lexington, Massachusetts, and elsewhere before the colonies declared their independence from Great Britain in 1776.

British Acts

King George III and the British **Parliament** felt colonists in North America should help pay for the French and Indian War and the protection provided by British troops. Great Britain began to pass acts (laws) that required the colonists to pay taxes. These included the **Sugar Act** in 1764, the **Stamp Act** in 1765, the **Townshend Acts** of 1767, the **Tea Act** of 1773, and the **Intolerable Acts** of 1774. The colonies responded by protesting and **boycotting** British goods. Colonists also formed groups such as the **Sons of Liberty** to take action against the acts.

Events turned violent in Boston in 1770. British troops fired on a rowdy crowd that was protesting British taxes. Samuel Adams called it the "Boston Massacre." He used the event to gain support for American independence. The colonists continued to protest British taxes. The king ordered General Thomas Gage to use military force to keep control in Massachusetts. In 1775, months before the signing of the Declaration of Independence, the Revolutionary War began.

KEY

- Locations with British troops in place

0   50   100 miles
0   50   100 kilometers

Quebec

CANADA

St. Lawrence River

Lake Champlain

MAINE
(part of Massachusetts)

VERMONT
Claimed by
NY & NH
at the time

Fort Ticonderoga

Lake Ontario

NEW HAMPSHIRE

NEW YORK

Albany

MASSACHUSETTS

Hudson River

CONNECTICUT

RHODE ISLAND

PENNSYLVANIA

NEW JERSEY

ATLANTIC OCEAN

Most fighting in the Revolutionary War took place in the northern colonies. The earliest fighting happened in Massachusetts, New York, and Canada in 1775.

What Was the British Army Like in 1775?

At the beginning of the Revolutionary War, in 1775, the British Army was considered one of the strongest in the world.

Officers

For most officers, being a soldier was their full-time job. Most officers came from the British upper class (wealthy). They purchased their **commissions**. This means they paid money for their place as an officer in the British Army, rather than earning it by gaining experience and doing a good job. Nonetheless, some British officers were highly experienced and good leaders.

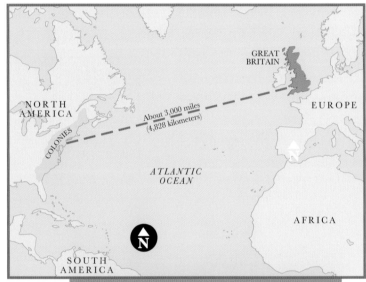

Great Britain wanted to protect its faraway colonies. There were about 8,000 British troops in North America when the Revolutionary War began in 1775.

Enlisted Men

Enlisted men were servicemen who were not officers. Enlisted men in the British Army were mostly from the lower levels of British society. They joined the army for various reasons. It provided a steady job and pay, as well as the chance for adventure. Most soldiers joined the army between age 17 and 25, though some were younger or older. About 80 percent of the British Army was **infantry**, or foot soldiers. Most of the rest were **cavalry**, or troops mounted on horseback.

Organization

A company of soldiers usually included about 40 men. They were under the command of a captain or other **commissioned officer**. A lieutenant and several **non-commissioned officers** assisted the captain. Nine or more companies made a battalion or regiment. So a regiment had about 400 men. Regiments were named for their number, for instance the "5th Regiment." A colonel was in charge of a regiment.

RANKS OF THE BRITISH ARMY

Below is a list of major ranks in the British Army during the Revolutionary War, from highest to lowest:

Commissioned Officers (COs)
general
lieutenant general
major general
brigadier general
colonel
lieutenant colonel
major
captain
lieutenant
ensign (or cornet in the cavalry)

Non-Commissioned Officers (NCOs)
sergeant
corporal
private

The uniform of a British soldier included a hat, shirt, waistcoat, white breeches (short pants), gaiters (leggings between the knee and shoe), shoes, and a red coat. Soldiers also received a Brown Bess musket.

Recruitment

In the 1770s, the British were involved in conflicts around the world. They needed troops in many places. The Recruiting Acts of 1778 and 1779 were passed to fill the ranks of the British Army. They allowed men who were unemployed or not considered responsible citizens to be forced to join the army. Many men volunteered because of the threat of being forced into the army. The British Army increased in size from 48,000 to 110,000 between 1775 and 1781.

GRENADIERS

Grenadiers were British soldiers trained to throw **grenades** at the enemy, which is how they got their name. By 1775, grenadiers were considered the best of the British troops. They were usually larger men, and appeared even larger because of the tall hats they wore. Each British regiment had a group of grenadiers.

Soldiers marched in columns to the beat of drums. In combat, they fought shoulder to shoulder in a battle line. A well-trained British soldier held the line and could shoot three to four times a minute.

When British troops fired on a Boston crowd in 1770, Samuel Adams called it the "Boston Massacre." However, future president John Adams defended the British soldiers in court. He proved they were threatened by the violent crowd and acted in self-defense.

Thinking About the Source:

What's happening in this image?

If someone made this image today, what would be different?

Loyalist Volunteers

The British Army recruited **Loyalist** volunteers in the **colonies**. About one-third of the colonial population stayed loyal to Great Britain. The British sometimes promised these colonists land in exchange for their service. Thousands of Loyalists fought for the British. British officer Banastre Tarleton created a successful Loyalist **cavalry** force.

CRIMINAL SOLDIERS?

Because soldiers were needed, British judges sometimes offered criminals the choice of joining the army instead of going to prison.

Harsh Discipline

The British Army was run with strict discipline. Flogging was the punishment a soldier received for failing to obey an order or follow rules. This meant the soldier would be brutally whipped. Some British regiments had nicknames such as "bloody backs" and "steel backs" because of the floggings their men received.

How Did the Continental Army Form?

Early in the Revolutionary War, the Americans did not have an official army or system of command. **Militias**, made up of citizen soldiers from the **colonies**, fought against the British. In June 1775, the **Continental Congress** approved the formation of the Continental Army.

Army Organization

The structure of the Continental Army was generally taken from the British Army. Companies were supposed to have about 80 men. A captain was usually in charge of the company, with a lieutenant and **ensign** to assist him. Companies also usually had 3–4 sergeants, 3–4 corporals, 60–70 privates, and a **fifer** and drummer if available.

About four to eight companies formed a battalion. About eight companies (one to two battalions) formed a regiment, with a colonel in charge. A lieutenant colonel and major assisted him. Regiments were formed into brigades, commanded by a brigadier general. Brigades were formed into divisions, which were usually commanded by a major general. At first, soldiers elected the other officers. Later, General George Washington appointed them.

The Continental Army depended on volunteer soldiers. They used posters to try to attract new soldiers.

TO ALL BRAVE, HEALTHY, ABLE BODIED, AND WELL DISPOSED YOUNG MEN, IN THIS NEIGHBOURHOOD, WHO HAVE ANY INCLINATION TO JOIN THE TROOPS, NOW RAISING UNDER GENERAL WASHINGTON, FOR THE DEFENCE OF THE LIBERTIES AND INDEPENDENCE OF THE UNITED STATES, Against the hostile designs of foreign enemies,

TAKE NOTICE,

Enlisting Continental Soldiers

The Continental Army had a hard time recruiting enough men to fight. In 1776, only 8,212 men had joined the army, even though Congress had authorized it to have up to 20,372. Congress then set **quotas** for each state and could **draft** men if necessary. At first, soldiers **enlisted** for one year.

RANKS OF THE CONTINENTAL ARMY

Below is a list of major ranks in the Continental Army during the Revolutionary War, from highest to lowest. The organization was basically taken from the British system.

Commissioned Officers (COs)
commander in chief (George Washington)
general
major general
brigadier general
colonel
lieutenant colonel
major
captain
lieutenant
ensign (second lieutenant)

Non-Commissioned Officers (NCOs)
sergeant
corporal
private

In 1779, the Continental Army chose a single official color for its uniforms. **Infantry** coats were blue, with a different color trim to identify the particular state or region.

Building the Army

On September 16, 1776, the **Continental Congress** decided to expand the Continental Army. It called for 88 battalions to serve for three years, or until the war ended. When there were not enough volunteers, states offered rewards of money and land to those who joined. However, they still could not fill the **quotas**. Some states recruited slaves by promising them freedom in return for their service.

An Undisciplined Army

When Washington arrived near Boston to take control of the Continental Army, he realized how difficult his task would be. The army was really just a collection of state **militias** made up of volunteers. There was no discipline or training. Most of the men were young and had no experience fighting. Troops were leaving when their **enlistment** ended and could not be convinced to stay. There was little respect for commanding officers and their orders.

Washington was worried when he saw his army. He wrote: "I should not be at all surprised at any disaster that may happen…"

Boys Fighting

Some Continental soldiers were 15 years old, or even younger. A ten-year-old boy named Israel Trask volunteered for the army along with his father. He served as a messenger and cook's helper. Joseph Plumb Martin was 15 when he volunteered for the Continental Army in July 1776. He kept a diary of his experiences as a soldier.

WAR LETTERS

John Greenwood was 16 years old. In 1775, he walked 241 kilometers (150 miles) alone to Boston to join the Continental Army. He stopped at taverns along the way and played tunes on his **fife**. He later remembered:

"They used to ask me where I came from and where I was going to, and when I told them I was going to fight for my country, they were astonished such a little boy, and alone, should have such courage."

It took discipline and experienced commanders to hold the line during battle. Militiamen were often very young and had little training.

Who Else Fought in the Revolution?

The British could not recruit enough soldiers in their own country and in the **colonies** to protect all their **territories**. They hired troops from other countries. Most troops were hired from the German state of Hesse-Cassel. These men, called Hessians, were experienced and disciplined soldiers. Almost 17,000 Hessians fought for the British.

In total, six German states sent nearly 30,000 soldiers to help the British fight in the Revolutionary War. The first Hessian troops landed in New York in August 1776. They fought in all parts of the colonies throughout the war. At the end of the war, some of these soldiers chose to stay in the United States. Others went to live in Canada or returned home.

Hessian soldiers found that their uniforms were not made for the American climate. Many Hessians made changes to their uniforms during the war.

The armies of the German states were well trained and successful. They had a strong sense of loyalty to their prince and country. Many of them viewed the colonial troops as rebels, with no sense of loyalty to their king. Many Hessian troops were amazed at how well the colonists lived in America, and how rich the land was in the colonies.

Other Continental Forces

Many Continental forces during the Revolutionary War had unique qualities and loyalties. The Minutemen of Massachusetts were ready to fight the British on a minute's notice. There were the Green Mountain Boys in New Hampshire, commanded by Ethan Allen. Marion's Men fought against British occupation in the South. They were named for their leader, Francis Marion. He was called the "Swamp Fox" for his ability to strike at the British Army, and then quickly slip away into the swamps of South Carolina.

Minutemen were picked, or volunteered, from the ranks of the militias.

Long Knives and Frontier Riflemen

The Long Knives of Kentucky and Virginia were named for the long hunting knives they carried. In 1778, George Rogers Clark led 200 Long Knives into the western **frontier**. This area is what is now considered the Midwestern United States. The Long Knives fought Native Americans who were British allies. They also helped capture British forts and trading posts.

The American frontier was a hard place to live. Frontier riflemen were tough and knew how to survive in the wilderness as well as the Native Americans. They usually carried a tomahawk (throwing axe) and a long hunting knife. They also carried long rifles and often acted as **sharpshooters** and **scouts**. Their knowledge of the woods and countryside allowed them to **ambush** enemy soldiers.

George Rogers Clark led his men on a difficult, rainy journey to attack the British at Vincennes, in what is now Indiana, in early 1779.

Americans fought against Mohawk warriors and British soldiers at the Battle of Oriskany on August 6, 1777.

Native Americans

Native Americans often clashed with **colonial** settlers, who continued to move west and claim more land. When the Revolutionary War began, most Native Americans who fought joined the British side. A few fought for the Continental Army. However, many tribes wanted to stay out of the fighting.

In the north and northwest, the Iroquois tribes first voted to remain neutral (not choose a side). Joseph Brant, a Mohawk chief, eventually convinced four of the six Iroquois tribes to support the British. The other two tribes fought for the colonists. In the South, the Cherokee were divided on whether or not to get involved. Some Cherokee warriors wanted to fight for the British. They launched raids (attacks) against colonial settlers. A force of 6,000 soldiers from four colonies took revenge on the Cherokee.

As a result of the Revolutionary War, Native Americans suffered even more and lost more of their territory. Colonists continued to settle farther west into the countryside, claiming more tribal lands and resources. The Native American way of life struggled to survive.

Black Soldiers

For a time during the Revolutionary War, blacks were not allowed to join the Continental Army. On the British side, freedom was promised to slaves who left their masters to fight for the king. Hundreds of slaves escaped to the British side. Some fought and did receive their freedom. Others were forced back into slavery after the war. Even though blacks were not officially allowed to join the Continental Army, many still served in the **colonial militias**.

The Black Regiment

With the need for more troops, some colonies began recruiting black soldiers. In February 1778, Rhode Island created a new 1st regiment. Free blacks and slaves were allowed to join, as well as Native Americans. Rhode Island paid owners for their slaves. Black volunteers received the same pay as white soldiers. More importantly, they were given their freedom. The Black Regiment of Rhode Island successfully fought against professional British and Hessian forces in the war.

France Enters the War

The Continental Army received help from individual European volunteers. However, more help was needed to successfully fight the British Army. Benjamin Franklin went to France to convince King Louis XVI (16th) to join the war against Britain. When word came of the Continental victory at Saratoga in 1777, France officially entered the war. More than 5,500 French troops fought in America under the command of Jean Baptiste Donatien de Vimeur, Comte de Rochambeau.

The most important contribution France made to the war was its navy. The small Continental fleet of ships could not stand up to the British Navy. The French fleet, under the command of Admiral Francois Joseph Paul, Comte de Grasse, prevented the British from receiving aid or escaping by sea in Virginia at the battle of Yorktown. The British were forced to surrender. This American victory secured colonial independence. It would not have been possible without the help of the French.

This was what a typical French soldier of the 1770s looked like.

What Weapons and Equipment Did Soldiers Use?

The flintlock musket was the weapon used by both armies in the Revolutionary War. The British "Brown Bess" was the most common musket used. It was deadly at close range. The Brown Bess was about one meter long (42 inches) and weighed about 6.4 kilograms (14 pounds). It was a muzzle-loading gun. This means it was loaded from the end, or muzzle, of the barrel. It used black powder (gunpowder) and shot musket balls.

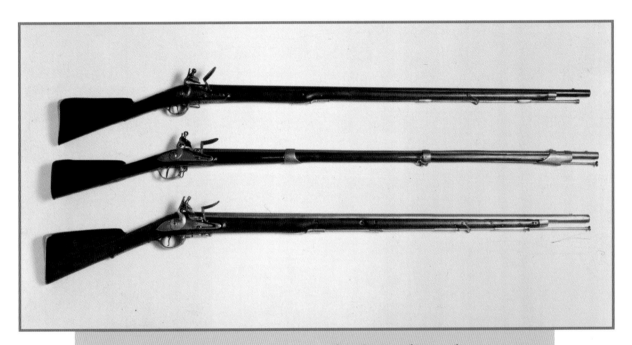

Primary Source: The "Brown Bess"

All three of these muskets were used in the Revolutionary War. The British "Brown Bess" (bottom) was the most commonly used musket in the Revolutionary War.

Thinking About the Source:

What do you notice first about the Brown Bess?

What can you learn from examining this image?

Firing the Musket

To aim or point the musket, soldiers just looked down the barrel. Pulling the trigger caused the flintlock to strike, which lit the powder in the **flash pan**. This ignited, or set fire to, the charge inside the bottom of the barrel. The musket ball then fired with a flash and loud bang, as well as a lot of smoke. Battlefields were full of smoke and the smell of gunpowder. Muskets quickly became dirty from the black powder and eventually had to be cleaned.

Cartridges

The armies used paper **cartridges**. A musket ball and the correct amount of black powder were put into a tube-shaped paper cartridge. The cartridge was then sealed, usually by tying it with string. Paper cartridges helped speed up the loading process. They also reduced the risk of loose powder being around sparking guns.

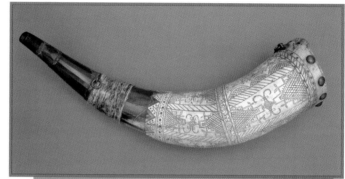

Soldiers carried cartridges, but many also carried extra black powder in a horn like this.

FIRING PROCEDURE

It took several steps to fire a musket:

- Rip the cartridge open with one's teeth
- Pour a small amount of powder into the flash pan
- Hold the musket so the end of the barrel is up
- Pour the remaining powder down the barrel, followed by the cartridge paper
- Put the musket ball down the barrel using the **ramrod**
- Raise the musket to firing position
- Pull back the hammer
- Aim or point and fire

Close Combat

Modern guns have rifling. Rifling is spiral-like grooves inside the barrel, which spin the bullet when it is shot. This makes the bullet fly farther and more accurately toward the target. The musket was smoothbored, which means it had no rifling. This made it less accurate. Bullets did not always fly straight, and they fell after a distance.

A **bayonet** could be attached to the end of the musket for close hand-to-hand fighting. Bayonets were used in a charge against the enemy. Because the musket was less accurate after 46 meters (50 yards), the bayonet was often a more effective weapon. Bayonets could also be used to defend against cavalry.

Cavalry

Riding horses, cavalry soldiers could travel long distances quickly and attack without warning. The saber (sword) was the most effective weapon of the cavalry rider. Horsemen also carried pistols. Cavalry units were called dragoons. Cavalry could give an army a big advantage in a battle. However, neither side had many cavalry units during the Revolutionary War. Horses were expensive and often hard to find.

If the British had more cavalry available, it may have changed the outcome of the Revolutionary War.

Continental cavalry units, called legions, included some mounted troops and some troops on foot. Lee's Legion, commanded by Colonel Henry "Light Horse Harry" Lee, was one of the most famous units. British cavalry protected the British troops when they marched from place to place. Lieutenant Colonel Banastre Tarleton was a famous British cavalry leader during the Revolutionary War. He recruited **Loyalists** and became known for his brutal treatment of enemies.

Both armies had drummers in their companies or regiments. Different drum calls were used to give orders on the battlefield. Drummers in the Continental Army were usually very young.

Artillery

In both armies, soldiers called gunners or bombardiers were trained to fire cannons called **artillery**. The men, cannons, equipment, and horses together were called a **battery**. A crew of soldiers firing a cannon had to find the target, guess the distance, and select the proper ammunition. Cannons could fire either a solid ball or various forms of shot, including grape shot. Grape shot was iron or lead balls about 2.5 centimeters (one inch) around.

Depending on their power and the ammunition used, cannons had a range (distance) of several hundred yards. Artillery fire could destroy attacking troops moving across open ground or protect troops defending a fixed position. The size of artillery was determined by the weight of the shells. Shells could weigh up to 11 kilograms (24 pounds).

Cannons were made of cast iron or brass and were very heavy. They could be attached to two-wheeled wooden frames for horses or oxen to pull.

Defending and Attacking Forts

Garrison and siege artillery were larger types of cannons. Garrison, or fortress, cannons were positioned to protect a fort from an attacking army. They were also used to control important positions on rivers and lakes. Siege cannons were heavy and large, and were not moved easily. They fired larger cannonballs that traveled longer distances. Siege cannons were used to attack defenses and buildings.

Henry Knox was selected as Chief of Artillery of the Continental Army. He learned about artillery from reading British military books on the subject.

What Was Fighting Like During the Revolution?

British Tactics

Because shooting was not always accurate, soldiers fired **volleys**. This meant they fired at the same time, on command, shooting a mass of musket balls at the enemy. To do this, soldiers had to be well trained to work together and follow orders. The British Army practiced firing volleys and was very good at it. On the battlefield, they formed into units two or three lines deep, shoulder to shoulder. An officer gave the order to load, fire, or move.

After firing several volleys to break up the enemy line, troops would charge with bayonets in order to drive the enemy forces from the battlefield.

A Real American Rifle Man

Soldiers had to remain calm through the noise and smoke, even while their fellow soldiers were falling and dying around them. They were expected to stand in line through the long process of reloading and firing their muskets, even when an enemy was quickly approaching from only yards away. The idea of this style of fighting was to break up the enemy's organized lines with volleys of fire, and then charge forward with **bayonets** to clear the enemy from the field.

Difficult Marching

Soldiers suffered through many hardships during the Revolutionary War. The fighting and battles were horrible. Soldiers also faced long marches to move from place to place in between fighting. They often lacked supplies and had to deal with harsh weather.

The challenges soldiers faced in between battles were often worse than the actual fighting. The Continental attack of Quebec, Canada, in 1775–1776 was a failure. The march to and from Canada, through the American wilderness, was even worse than the fighting. The winter weather was harsh. Continental soldiers could not find food. At one point, men were desperate enough to boil and eat candles. Many soldiers died of disease or starvation.

WAR LETTERS

Individual soldiers dealt with death and the pressure of battle differently. A British observer named Nicholas Cresswell described part of a battle in New York in 1777:

> "I never before saw such a shocking scene: some dead, others dying, death in different shapes; some of the wounded making the most pitiful lamentations [wailing sounds], others that were of different parties cursing each other…"

Some soldiers panicked and fled when faced with fighting. Garret Watts of North Carolina wrote of his experience in a battle against the British:

> "I confess I was amongst the first that fled. The cause of that I cannot tell, except that everyone I saw was about to do the same. It was instantaneous. There was no effort to rally, no encouragement to fight. Officers and men joined in the flight. I threw away my gun, and, reflecting I might be punished for being found without arms [weapons], I picked up a drum, which gave forth such a sound when touched by twigs I cast it away."

Fighting in the Revolutionary War could be brutal and confusing. The fight pictured here took place at the Chew House during the Battle of Germantown, Pennsylania, in 1777.

Harsh Weather, Lack of Supplies

George Washington earned a much-needed victory with his surprise attack at Trenton, New Jersey, in December 1776. However, the condition of his army was poor. Troops suffered through winter weather without proper gear and supplies. Colonel John Fitzgerald was an **aide** to Washington. He recorded what happened on December 25, as the army prepared to cross the Delaware River into New Jersey:

"The regiments…are marching toward the ferry. It is fearfully cold and raw, and a snowstorm setting in. The wind is northeast and beats in the faces of the men. It will be a terrible night for the soldiers who have no shoes. Some of them have tied old rags around their feet; others are barefoot…"

Washington and Lafayette, the French commander, are pictured here on horseback at snowy Valley Forge. Troops huddle near a fire in the background for warmth.

Winter at Valley Forge

The following December, Washington and his army settled at Valley Forge in Pennsylvania for the winter. Some soldiers finished the term of their **enlistment** at the end of the year. They wanted to go home. However, General Washington inspired many men to stick it out. They continued to lack food and supplies through the winter. However, they also received military training from Baron von Steuben, a Prussian volunteer. The army that made it through the winter at Valley Forge emerged as a much better fighting force. It was prepared to face the British Army in open battle.

WAR LETTERS

A Continental sergeant known only as "Sergeant R——" also wrote of the hardships:

> "At this time our troops were in a destitute [poor] and deplorable [dreadful] condition. The horses attached to our cannon were without shoes, and when passing over the ice they would slide in every direction and could advance only by the assistance of the soldiers. Our men, too, were without shoes or other comfortable clothing; and as traces of our march towards Princeton, the ground was literally marked with the blood of the soldiers' feet."

Despite the fact that he spoke no English, Baron von Steuben successfully organized and trained Washington's army at Valley Forge.

What Was Medicine Like?

In the 1770s, most physicians (doctors) in America learned their skills as apprentices. This means they learned for many years from other physicians with more experience. Some also went to medical college in one of the cities. Continental military hospitals were short on medicine, food, and supplies. Conditions were horrible. Physicians often had to remove bullets and amputate (cut off) limbs. Soldiers suffered, because there was no **anesthesia** to stop the pain at that time.

Medicine was still primitive during the Revolutionary War. Army hospitals were dirty and filled with the suffering wounded. Soldiers often felt like they had a better chance of surviving on the battlefield than in the hospital.

Illness

Many men died of diseases such as **smallpox** and **dysentery**. Most illnesses were caused by unsanitary, or unclean, conditions in the camps. Physicians did not know about germs and viruses, or how diseases spread. Surgical tools were often not even washed between uses. Bandages were sometimes even reused. A soldier with even a minor wound could catch an infection and die.

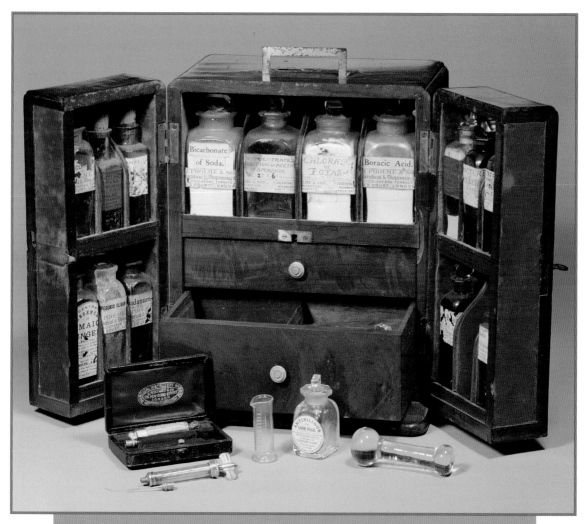

Medicines of the time included herbal remedies, powders, and chemical mixtures. In the Revolutionary War, only a little more than one out of three soldiers who needed an amputation lived.

British vs. American

Dr. Benjamin Rush was a physician and politician. He served as a medical administrator in the Continental Army. He later left his job because he was frustrated with how poorly the hospital department was run. While in Trenton, New Jersey, on October 1, 1777, Rush wrote a letter to John Adams. He praised the order and cleanliness of the camps and hospitals of the British Army compared to those of the Continental Army:

"They [the British] pay a supreme regard to the cleanliness and health of their men…There is the utmost order and contentment in their hospitals. The wounded whom we brought off from the field were not half so well treated as those whom we left in [British] General Howe's hands. Our officers and soldiers spoke with gratitude and affection of their surgeons…It would take a volume to tell you of the many things I saw and heard which tend to show the extreme regard that our enemies pay to discipline, order, economy and cleanliness among their soldiers."

Physicians and nurses in Continental Army hospitals did all they could for wounded and sick soldiers. There were simply not enough doctors and very few medical supplies.

Dr. Benjamin Rush was also a member of the Continental Congress and a signer of the Declaration of Independence.

SMALLPOX

Disease killed many more soldiers than bullets or **bayonets** in the Revolutionary War. Symptoms of smallpox included a high fever, back pain, and skin eruptions. Those who survived had permanent scars. But they were also **immune** to the disease after having it. George Washington survived smallpox when he was 19 years old. He had visible scars the rest of his life as a result. The smallpox **inoculation** existed at the time, but not everyone was convinced of how useful it was. Washington strongly believed inoculation worked. He created a system where new recruits to the army would immediately be inoculated with smallpox.

WAR LETTERS

Conditions for the wounded were terrible. Dr. Lewis Beebe of Massachusetts described an experience with the Continental Army in 1776:

"Was struck with amazement upon my arrival to see the vast crowds of poor distressed creatures…Scarcely a tent upon this isle but what contains one or more in distress and continually groaning and calling for relief…The most shocking of all spectacles was to see a large barn crowded full of men…many of which could not see, speak or walk…No mortal will ever believe what these suffered unless they were eyewitnesses."

Women served as nurses during the war. They tended to the wounded on the battlefields and at camp hospitals.

What Was Fighting Like at Sea?

During the Revolutionary War, most Americans lived within 161 kilometers (100 miles) of the ocean. The people and armies depended on the sea for transportation and necessary supplies. Many colonists made a living from the sea, as traders, fishermen, or shipbuilders. The **colonies** did not have the money to purchase new warships to fight the British in 1775. Instead, they turned merchant ships into warships by mounting guns on them.

British Navy

The few ships of the newly formed Continental Navy were no match for the British Navy. British warships were faster and easier to move than merchant ships. British crews were better trained and in better health than those of the Continental Navy. British warships sailed the waters near the North American colonies without fear of the Continental Navy.

French Navy

France entered the war in 1778. The French Navy gave the colonists the sea power needed to confront British warships. Without the French Navy, the colonial victory at the battle of Yorktown in 1781 would not have been possible.

Ships in Battle

One of the common battle strategies at this time was for ships to sail next to each other and fire their cannons. Destroying a ship's sails limited its movement. The attacking ship then sailed across the bow (front) or stern (rear) of the disabled ship and fired again. The attacking crew then boarded the disabled ship and captured its remaining crew.

Privateers

During the Revolutionary War, the British Navy **blockaded** colonial ports. Privateers attacked British ships bringing supplies to the colonies. Privateers were armed ships that were not in the navy, but attacked and robbed enemy ships. The men who sailed on those ships were also called privateers. Hundreds of privateers attacked British merchant ships during the war. They did about $18 million in damage to British business.

John Paul Jones defeated the British warship *Serapis* off the coast of England at the Battle of Flamborough Head in 1779.

Diversity on Colonial Ships

In the 1700s, both free blacks and runaway slaves found work in the shipping and fishing industries in New England. Many of them became privateers when the Revolutionary War began in 1775. The Continental Navy also welcomed blacks. Hundreds of blacks served on the seas during the war, and most Continental crews included several black men.

Impressment

Impressment is the act of forcing, or pressing, men to serve in the navy. This was a common practice for the British Navy in the 1700s. The Continental Navy also used impressment. When crews were taken from merchant ships, they were forced to serve in the navy. This was because sailors were badly needed for naval ships. Conditions were poor, and many sailors deserted (ran away). Impressment was a way to fill the ships with sailing men.

The British also used ships to hold prisoners during the Revolutionary War. The British prison ship HMS *Jersey* is pictured here anchored near Brooklyn during the British occupation of New York.

Prisoners of War

The British kept ships anchored in New York Harbor to serve as prisons during the Revolutionary War. Thousands of captured Americans were crowded onto these ships. Conditions were awful, with overcrowding, very little food, and no medical care. Thousands of prisoners died, mostly from disease.

The number of cannons that ships carried usually determined their size. Some large British warships had 60 cannons or more.

WAR LETTERS

William Slade was a Connecticut boy who fought for the Continental Army. He was captured by the British at Fort Washington in 1776 and taken to the *Grosvenor*, which was a prison ship. He wrote of his experience:

"Saturday, 14th [December 1776]. Times look dark. Deaths prevail among us...

Tuesday, 17th. Suffer with cold and hunger. We are treated worse than cattle and hogs...

Sunday, 22nd. Last night nothing but grones all night of sick and dying...Deaths multiply...Weather cold...Had nothing but sorrow and sadness...

Monday, 23rd...Times look very dark...One dies almost every day...People gone bad with the pox.

Friday, 27th. Three men of our battalion died last night...Small pox increases fast."

What Was Life Like in Camp?

During the Revolutionary War, armies made camp when they weren't marching or fighting. Armies usually camped for the winter, and then continued fighting in the spring. While camped, soldiers marched in drills and trained for combat. They repaired equipment and made more bullets (musket balls). Soldiers who were wounded or ill were treated in camp hospitals.

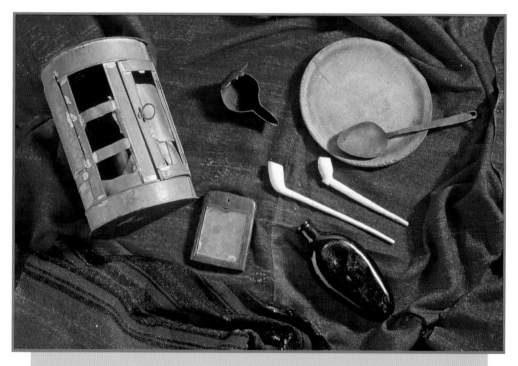

**Primary Source:
Soldiers Artifacts**

Soldiers used simple tools, but everything had to be carried on long marches. From top left are: tin lantern; wrought iron open lamp; wooden plate; forged iron tablespoon; white clay pipes; medicine bottle; mirror.

Thinking About the Source:

What do you notice first about these items?

Why do you think all of these items were important?

Feeding the Soldiers

It was common for locals to gather and sell produce to the soldiers, creating a market in the camp. British commanders were used to these camp markets from experiences in Europe and elsewhere. They often relied on them to feed their troops. However, they didn't realize how few people lived in areas of the American countryside. For that reason, the British Army sometimes suffered from a lack of food and supplies, just as the Continental Army did.

The Continental Army often did not have money to purchase food for the soldiers. The **Continental Congress** created Continental money to use instead of British currency. However, it had little value, which made food very expensive. Farmers and merchants did not always accept **colonial** paper money. Hungry soldiers were forced to search for food in the surrounding fields and forests. This is known as foraging.

WAR LETTERS

Joseph Plumb Martin wrote about his experience foraging for food while the army was camped for the winter:

"With a small group of men, I was ordered to leave our quarters to go on foraging duty. This meant we would roam through the countryside for many weeks seeking food for the army…Our duty was to load the wagons with hay, corn, meal, or whatever and to keep them company till they arrived safely…I had to travel far and near, in cold and in storms, by day and by night…"

This is a five-dollar Continental banknote from 1775. As the war went on, Continental money was worth less and less.

Women at Camp

During the Revolutionary War, some women and their children could be found at both the Continental and British Army camps. Many women had no choice. They were widows or wives who faced starvation if left at home. Others had fled cities like Boston and Philadelphia when the British took control.

These women and children were known as camp followers. They traveled with the troops and helped by doing laundry, mending clothes, cooking, and acting as nurses for the wounded. During battles they carried messages and supplies, and sometimes assisted with the **artillery**.

It is believed that nearly 20,000 women were camp followers during the Revolutionary War. Many brought their small children, and some even gave birth while traveling with the army.

Valley Forge

During the winter of 1777–1778, Washington's army camped at Valley Forge in Pennsylvania. The soldiers did not have enough food and supplies. However, the Continental soldiers trained hard that winter under the guidance of the Prussian Baron von Steuben. It was a turning point for the Continental Army. By the end of the winter, Washington's soldiers were prepared to fight the British Army. News came early in 1778 that the French entered the war against the British. There was new hope for the cause of independence.

WAR LETTERS

Sarah Osborn married a blacksmith who **enlisted** in the Continental Army. He insisted she come along, and Sarah was a camp follower for three years. She later told of her experience at the Battle of Yorktown:

"On one occasion when [Sarah] was thus employed carrying in provisions, she met General Washington, who asked her if she 'was not afraid of the cannonballs'? She replied, 'No...' that 'It would not do for the men to fight and starve, too.'"

Camp life was difficult. Here, Continental soldiers at Valley Forge are shown trying to keep warm by the fire. In the background, others gather more wood.

Timeline

1754–1763	French and Indian War
1764	Sugar Act passed
1765	Stamp Act passed
1765	Quartering Act passed
	Sons of Liberty formed
1766	Stamp Act repealed
	Parliament passes Declaratory Acts
1767	Townshend Acts passed
1768	British troops in Boston
1770	Boston Massacre (March 5)
1772	Boston Committee of Correspondence formed
1773	Tea Act passed
	Boston Tea Party (December 16)
1774	Coercive Acts (Intolerable Acts) passed
	First Continental Congress meets
1775	Paul Revere and William Dawes warn colonists that the British are coming
	Battles of Lexington and Concord (April 19)
	Second Continental Congress meets
	George Washington appointed commander of Continental Army
	Battle of Bunker Hill (June 17)
	Defeat at Quebec (December 30)
1776	Thomas Paine writes *Common Sense*
	Siege of Boston ends
	Declaration of Independence signed (July 4)
	New York falls to the British
	Battle of Trenton, New Jersey (December 26)
1777	Battle of Princeton, New Jersey (January 3)
	Fort Ticonderoga falls to the British (July 5)
	Battle of Bennington (August 16)
	Battle of Brandywine (September 11)

	Philadelphia falls to the British (September 26)
	Battle of Germantown (October 4)
	Battle of Saratoga (October 7)
	British General Burgoyne surrenders (October 17)
	Congress passes Articles of Confederation (November 15)
	Winter of Washington's army at Valley Forge
1778	France declares war and joins the Patriot cause
	Battle of Monmouth Courthouse (June 28)
	Savannah captured by the British (December 29)
1779	George Rogers Clark captures Vincennes (February 25) in the Western frontier
	Naval battle of John Paul Jones's *Bonhomme Richard* against the British warship *Serapis* (September 23)
1780	Charleston, South Carolina, falls to the British (May 12)
	Battle of Camden (August 16)
	Battle of Kings Mountain (October 7)
1781	Battle of Cowpens (January 17)
	Articles of Confederation adopted by the states (March 1)
	Battle of Guilford Courthouse (March 15)
	Battle of Eutaw Springs (September 8)
	Cornwallis and the British surrender at Yorktown, Virginia (October 19)
1783	Treaty of Paris signed, ending the war (September 3)
	Continental Army disbanded, and Washington retires from the military
1785	Congress establishes dollar as official currency
1786	Shay's Rebellion
1787	Northwest Ordinance
	Constitutional Convention meets and Constitution signed (September 17)
1788	Federalist Papers
	Constitution is ratified
1789	First meeting of Congress
	George Washington sworn in as first president
1791	Congress adopts the Bill of Rights as the first ten amendments to the Constitution

Glossary

aide military staff that helps an officer of higher rank

ambush sudden attack on someone by people who have been hiding and waiting

anesthesia state of being unable to feel pain

artillery large guns such as cannons; the part of the army that uses the large guns

battery cannons, gunners (or bombardiers), equipment, and horses involved with the artillery

bayonet long knife that is attached to the end of a rifle

blockade surrounding of an area to stop people or supplies from leaving or entering

boycott refuse to buy something or do something

cartridge tube containing explosive powder and a bullet to put in a gun

cavalry part of an army that fights on horses

colony area that is under the political control of a more powerful country that is usually far away

commission position of an officer in the armed forces

commissioned officer (CO) position of authority in the military granted by a higher governing authority or king; commissioned officers are the commanding officers of military units

Continental Congress group of men who represented the thirteen colonies during the time of the Revolutionary War

draft order someone to join the armed forces

dysentery serious disease of the bowels

enlistment time in the military; to enlist is to join the military

ensign army officer similar to a second lieutenant

fife musical instrument like a small flute

flash pan small pan that held the initial charge of gunpowder for a flintlock musket

French and Indian War name for fighting that took place from 1754–1763 in North America between the French and the British

frontier area where not many people have lived before and not much is known about

grenade small bomb that can be thrown by hand

guerilla style of fighting where small groups attack and then escape, rather than facing the enemy in open battle

immune not affected by something, such as an illness

infantry foot soldiers of the army

inoculation weak form of a disease used to prevent the full form of the disease

Intolerable Acts name colonists gave to the Coercive Acts of 1774, which included several acts

Loyalist person who remained loyal to Great Britain during the Revolutionary War

militia group of people who act as soldiers but are not part of the permanent, professional army

non-commissioned officer (NCO) enlisted soldier holding some authority, usually obtained by being promoted

Parliament main lawmaking group in Great Britain

quota amount of something expected to be done

ramrod rod attached to the bottom of the barrel of a musket used to clean and push the gunpowder and shot into the barrel

scout soldier sent to search the area in front of an army to get information about the enemy

sharpshooter someone very skilled at aiming and shooting with a gun

smallpox serious disease that causes spots, which leave marks on the skin

Sons of Liberty secret groups formed in the colonies before the Revolutionary War that included people who protested British taxes and supported independence from Great Britain

Stamp Act act in 1765 that required a tax to be paid when paper documents were made or sold

Sugar Act act in 1764 that taxed molasses shipped to colonial ports and prevented the colonies from importing molasses from other countries

Tea Act act in 1773 that made the East India Company the only company allowed to sell tea in the American colonies, with Parliament collecting a tax on it

Townshend Acts acts in 1767 that placed taxes on items brought into the colonies, including glass, lead, paper, and tea

volley large number of bullets shot through the air at the same time

Find Out More

Books

Anderson, Dale. *Key Battles of the American Revolution, 1776–1778*. Milwaukee, WI: Gareth Stevens, 2005.

Castrovilla, Selene. *By the Sword: A Young Man Meets War*. Honesdale, PA: Calkins Creek, 2007.

Murray, Stuart. *American Revolution*. New York: DK Children, 2005.

Websites

http://www.historyforkids.org/learn/northamerica/after1500/history/revolution.htm
This site, run by Kidipede, provides all kinds of links discussing different ideas and events of the Revolutionary War.

http://www.pbs.org/ktca/liberty/
This PBS site discusses the American Revolution and matches a TV series aired by PBS called "Liberty! The American Revolution," which is also available on DVD.

DVDs

Liberty! The American Revolution (DVD). Hosted by news anchor Forrest Sawyer and narrated by Edward Herrmann. PBS DVD Video, 1997.

The Revolution (DVD). History Channel DVDs, 2006.

Index